How To Write Good Emails

The Ultimate Guide on How To Write Professional Emails

Patrick Anna

Table of Contents

Chapter 1

The Art of Effective Email Communication

In today's interconnected world, email is a critical component of professional communication. Whether you're a freelancer looking for new clients, a job seeker reaching out to possible employers, or a business professional looking to form partnerships, the ability to send good emails to people you don't know is an important talent. However, with the proliferation of spam filters and suspicious recipients, your well-intentioned emails may wind up in the spam folder, never to be viewed or read.

Mastering the art of reaching out to individuals without triggering spam filters requires finesse, strategy, and knowledge of email etiquette. The modern inbox is a battleground where legitimate emails compete for attention among a sea of spam. Email service providers use complex algorithms to analyze incoming emails for numerous signs before deciding their legitimacy and relevancy. When you send an email to someone you don't know, you go through these filters in the hopes of getting through to the recipient's principal inbox.

Your email's subject line serves as its gateway. It should be succinct, interesting, and relevant. Avoid employing too promotional language or gimmicky phrases that could set off spam filters. Instead, personalize the subject line by using the recipient's name or mentioning anything related to their interests or industry. Make the email's content as transparent as possible without being misleading.

Before you write your email, spend some time studying the recipient. Instead of welcoming them generically, call them by name. To develop a personal connection, refer to their most recent work, achievements, or mutual relationships. Genuine interest and relevancy will make your email stand out and show that you made an effort to grasp the recipient's history.

Clarity and Conciseness

From newsletters and social network updates to frauds and commercial advertising, our trained eye, peeking over the lip of a hot cup of morning coffee, has learned to distinguish between rubbish and legitimate emails.

While all of this is simple, sorting is a challenge. We usually classify emails into two categories: those that are urgent and require immediate action and those that are categorized as unimportant and put away to be reviewed later or never. How do you, as a frequent email recipient and sender, ensure that the emails you send do not fall into the latter category?

Sending a poorly worded email implies that you haven't considered what is important. And you're diminishing your chances of receiving a response. If it takes a lot of words to explain what you have in mind, give it more thought. As with face-to-face communication, using basic etiquette and manners in email conversations demonstrates respect and consideration for your recipient.

A good email should be brief, succinct, and only include the most important information. A lengthy communication with a needless backstory would be considered bad.

Subject headings serve the purpose of capturing the reader's attention and allowing them to determine whether or not to continue reading. Of course, it would be silly to print a newspaper without headlines, so never leave the subject line blank. The recipient can tell what the email is about with just a few carefully chosen phrases. Including a subject header increases the odds that your email will be viewed rather than removed as spam.

Long diatribes should be avoided in order to communicate effectively through email. Some people believe that offering a lot of backstory and extra details will make the message clearer to the recipient. On the contrary, creating long-winded emails tends to confuse and make responding to your word labyrinth difficult. Brevity is essential. You can encourage the respondent to be brief through your own brevity. Eliminating chatter will not only make you a better writer, but it will also improve your ability to deliver your intended message with the appropriate impact.

Do not ask too many inquiries. Even if you have a million burning queries, divide them into several emails. You'll have a better chance of receiving a response if you ask 2-3 questions rather than bombarding the recipient with question marks. Consider how many emails you've received that made you wonder what was in them! On the other end of the scale, consider how many times you've written an email that was back with a slew of questions because you didn't write properly.

Edit. I know we want to write it, send it, and then forget it. That's like telling the receiver they don't deserve a good email. We're not advising that you spend hours perfecting every email, but if you can take a few minutes to look over an email and delete extraneous sentences, words, and typos, you'll be doing your recipient and yourself a huge favor!

Chapter 2

The Effectiveness of a Strong Subject Line

However, given the sheer volume of emails we receive each day, it can be difficult to stand out in a packed inbox. An engaging email subject line can make a huge impact. The subject line is your first impression, the critical moment when the receiver decides whether or not to read your email.

In today's world, we are inundated with emails, and it's easy for our inboxes to become clogged with messages we don't want to see. A compelling subject line for an email can really make a difference. The subject line is the first thing your recipient sees, and it has a significant impact on whether or not they open your email. If your subject line does not capture their attention and persuade them to read on, your email will most likely be ignored or deleted.

An intriguing email subject line is vital because it is the recipient's initial impression of you. It can set the tone for the rest of your email by demonstrating your trustworthiness, authority, and professionalism. A smart subject line can also help you stand out in a congested inbox, increasing your email open rates. In fact, research has shown that emails with tailored subject lines are twenty-six percent more likely to be opened, while subject lines featuring numbers raise open rates by 15%.

However, a poorly composed subject line can have the opposite impact. If your subject line is dull, vague, or unhelpful, your recipient may decide to disregard your email. In some situations, a faulty subject line might make your email appear spammy, resulting in your message being filtered or categorized as junk mail.

In summary, the significance of an engaging email subject line cannot be emphasized. It can mean the difference between your email being read or ignored. So, take the time to create an intriguing, useful, and relevant subject line for your receiver. With a fantastic subject line, you can enhance your chances of receiving a response and reaching your goal.

Understanding Your Audience and Purpose

When it comes to creating captivating email subject lines, one of the most critical considerations is your target audience and purpose. The subject line you create should be specific to the recipient and the purpose you want to achieve with your email.

Understanding your audience is knowing who you are writing for and what their interests, preferences, and pain points are. For example, if you're contacting a potential customer, you might want to emphasize the advantages of your product or service and how it can address an issue they're having. If you're emailing a coworker, however, you should focus on the specific task or project at hand and how your email can help move things forward.

In addition to identifying your target, you should be clear about the objective of your email. After reading your message, what action do you want the recipient to take? Do you want them to perform a specific action, such as scheduling a meeting or making a purchase? Are you merely trying to supply them with information or an update? Being clear about your aim allows you to create a subject line that expresses your message concisely and compellingly.

Overall, understanding your audience and objective is essential for producing great email subject lines. By personalizing your subject line to the recipient and the goal you're attempting to achieve, you can boost the likelihood of your email being opened and receiving the reaction you desire.

Keeping It Short and Sweet

One of the most crucial components of creating an effective email subject line is keeping it brief and sweet. People are busy and have short attention spans in today's fast-paced environment, so a long, unclear subject line is likely to be ignored. That is why your subject line should be as succinct and to the point as feasible.

The optimum subject line length varies based on the situation, but it should not exceed 50 characters. This ensures that the receiver can read the complete subject line without having it cut off, whether they are on a desktop computer or a mobile device.

To keep your subject line brief and simple, concentrate on the most crucial information you want to express. Try to use clear, detailed language that accurately conveys the message of your email. Avoid utilizing filler words or superfluous details in your topic line.

Using action-oriented verbs and strong phrases that convey a sense of urgency or excitement is an effective way to keep your subject line brief. For example, adding terms like "urgent," "important," or "limited time" might generate a sense of urgency and motivate the receiver to open your email immediately.

To summarize, keeping your email subject line brief and sweet is critical for getting your message over and capturing the recipient's attention. You may design a brief and attractive subject line by focusing on the most relevant information, utilizing plain language, and including action-oriented terms.

Using Numbers, Questions, and Personalization

There are various strategies for creating interesting email subject lines that will help your message stand out. The most effective strategies include the use of numbers, questions, and personalizing.

Using numbers in your subject line is an excellent method to capture the recipient's attention and lend credibility to your message. For example, you could utilize a number to emphasize a statistic or a feature of your product or service. Using numbers can also help to separate the information and make the subject line simpler to read.

Another successful method is to include questions in your subject line. This might be an excellent method to engage the recipient and entice them to read your email to discover the answer. When utilizing questions, ensure that they are relevant to the recipient and the objective of your email.

Finally, personalization can be an effective strategy for developing an engaging subject line. You can create a feeling of importance and connection by adding the recipient's name or other specific information, which will increase the probability that the email will be opened. Personalization allows you to personalize your subject line to the recipient's interests, desires, or location.

It's crucial to use these strategies sparingly and to make sure they are pertinent to the recipient and the goal of your email. Overdoing personalization can come across as obtrusive or unsettling while overusing numbers or questions can make your subject line appear spammy or gimmicky.

In conclusion, creating intriguing email subject lines can be accomplished with the help of techniques like personalization, questions, and numbers. You can boost the likelihood that your email will be opened and that the intended result will be reached by utilizing them in a pertinent and suitable manner.

The Influence of Scarcity and Urgency

Urgency and scarcity are two of the most potent psychological motivators in marketing. To convey a sense of urgency or scarcity, you might use these motivators in the subject line of your emails. A strong desire to act can arise from the perception that something is both significant and finite.

You can add urgency to your subject line by making it time-sensitive. Use words like "last chance" or "today only," for instance, to nudge the recipient to act right away. You can boost the perceived value of your email and persuade the recipient to open it immediately by instilling a sense of urgency.

On the other hand, emphasizing that something is in short supply or in high demand can help to create a sense of scarcity. Use words like "limited availability" or "going fast," for instance, to instill a sense of scarcity in relation to your good or service. You can boost the perceived value of your offer and motivate the recipient to act now, before it's too late, by doing this.

It's crucial to employ scarcity and urgency in your email subject lines in a responsible and sincere manner. Avoid inflating a sense of scarcity or urgency since this will undermine your credibility and reduce the likelihood that the recipient will continue to trust you. Rather, be truthful and open about how urgent or limited your offer is.

In conclusion, email subject lines that compel the recipient to act can be written by leveraging the power of urgency and scarcity. You can raise the perceived value of your offer and encourage the recipient to open your email and take the desired action by using a sense of urgency or scarcity in your subject line.

Steer Clear Of Spam Traps And Deceptive Subject Lines

It's crucial to steer clear of tactics in email subject lines that could confuse the recipient or set off spam filters. This is due to the fact that employing deceptive or spammy subject lines can harm your reputation, lessen the impact of your email marketing, and possibly result in legal repercussions.

Spam traps are one thing to be cautious of. Internet service providers (ISPs) and email security firms create these email addresses in an effort to identify and block spammers. Your sender's reputation may suffer and there's a greater chance that future emails you send will be flagged as spam if yours lands in a spam trap. Make sure your email list is current and that you are only sending emails to those who have given their consent to receive them in order to avoid falling victim to spam traps.

Moreover, steer clear of deceptive subject lines. This could involve making fictitious claims, making false promises, or creating attention-grabbing headlines that don't fairly sum up the content of your email. Although you may see a brief increase in open rates as a result, this can damage your reputation and reduce the likelihood that the recipient will continue to trust you. Make sure your subject accurately conveys the content of your email and that you are fulfilling any promises you make in order to avoid creating misleading subject lines.

Moreover, be aware of other typical spam triggers, like using all caps, specific trigger words like "free" or "urgent," or overuse of punctuation. Aim for clarity, conciseness, and relevancy in your subject line, and steer clear of any tactics that could give the impression that your email is spam.

By adhering to recommended practices, staying current with spam filter algorithms, and considering the requirements and preferences of the recipient, you can craft subject lines that not only encourage your audience to open your email but also foster credibility and trust.

Examining and Assessing the Subject Lines of Your Emails

It can be difficult to come up with intriguing email subject lines, and it's not always clear what will appeal to your target audience. To determine what works and what doesn't, it's crucial to test and measure your email subject lines.

Sending a small sample of your audience two or more versions of your email with distinct subject lines to each one is how you test the effectiveness of your subject lines. The open rates of each email can then be compared to determine which subject line was more successful. You can determine what kinds of subject lines work best for your specific audience by putting your subject lines to this kind of testing.

Monitoring the effectiveness of your subject lines over time is also crucial. You can use this to find patterns, trends, and areas that need work. You may observe, for instance, that subject lines containing questions outperform those without questions, or that subject lines containing emojis outperform those without on mobile devices.

You can use email marketing software that monitors metrics like open rates, click-through rates, and conversion rates to gauge how effective your subject lines are. This will help you gauge how well your subject lines encourage interaction and lead to conversions.

You can continuously enhance your email marketing efforts and make sure you're providing content that appeals to your audience by testing and measuring your email subject lines. In the end, this can help your business generate more revenue and conversions by strengthening your relationships with your subscribers and raising your open and click-through rates.

Subject lines that captivate your audience's attention and encourage them to take action can be created by being willing to experiment and try new ideas, as well as using statistics to influence your decisions.

Tips for Creating Effective Subject Lines in Different Situations

Writing great email subject lines is a critical skill for anyone looking to thrive in email marketing. However, best practices for creating subject lines differ based on the situation, audience, and goal of the email. Here are some suggestions for developing excellent subject lines in various situations:

Promotional emails

If you are sending a marketing email, such as a sales promotion or a discount offer, make sure the subject line clearly states the offer or benefit. Use numbers, urgency, and individuality to make the subject line more appealing.

Newsletters

When sending a newsletter, select a subject line that highlights the newsletter's most intriguing or valuable material. You can also use questions or teasers to encourage the reader to open the email.

Event Invitations

If you're inviting folks to an event, make sure the subject line clearly states the date, time, and location of the event. You can also utilize customization to make the subject line more interesting.

Follow-up email

If you're sending a follow-up email, like a reminder or a meeting invitation, make sure the subject line properly indicates the email's goal. Use urgency and customization to improve the subject line's effectiveness.

Transactional emails

Commercial emails, such as order confirmations or delivery alerts, should contain subject lines that clearly state the objective of the email. Make the subject line more relevant to the recipient by personalizing it and including order-specific facts.

In general, the key to crafting great subject lines in many scenarios is to be clear, brief, and targeted to the receiver. To make the subject line more appealing, utilize approaches such as customization, urgency, and questions, but avoid using false or spammy tactics that may harm your credibility. You can increase the effectiveness of your emails in boosting engagement and conversions by adapting your subject lines to the situation, audience, and goal of your email.

Examples of Effective Email Subject Lines.

Crafting a compelling email subject line might be difficult, but fortunately, there are plenty of examples to help you. Here are some examples of appealing email subject lines that will assist you in developing great subject lines for your own email campaigns:

'Limited-time offer: 50% off everything!'
This subject line conveys a sense of urgency and scarcity, prompting the receiver to open the email and take advantage of the offer before it expires.

'How to solve a problem under five minutes'
This subject line promises a quick and simple answer to an issue the reader may be facing, increasing the likelihood that they will open the email to learn more.

'You do not want miss out on this exclusive event'
This subject line conveys a sense of exclusivity, prompting the reader to open the email to discover more about the event and how to attend.

'Get [desired] with these [number] tips'
This subject line promises a desirable end and offers several tips to help the reader attain it, increasing the likelihood that they will open the email to learn more.

"Hello, [recipient's name], check out these [product/service] bargains, particularly for you!"
This subject line uses customization to convey closeness and relevancy, increasing the likelihood that the receiver will open the email and take advantage of the offers.

All things considered, the best email subject lines are those that use personalization to create a feeling of relevance and intimacy, communicate a sense of urgency or scarcity, promise a desirable outcome or solution, and are succinct and direct. By studying examples of intriguing email subject lines and applying them to your own email campaigns, you can boost the effectiveness of your email marketing efforts and increase engagement and conversions.

Chapter 3

Structuring Your Emails for Impact

A successful email is similar to the human body. It consists of several components that must all work together in order for it to function and perform properly as a unit. Every good email should have at least seven unique components that motivate consumers to open it, engage with the content, and eventually convert.

To get it properly and see that delicious ROI, these are the key components that make up the anatomy of a great email:

'From' Field

The "from" space is an important real estate element since it can immediately establish trust. Never set your email to be sent from a generic address. Instead, have the "from" line include the name of someone in your organization, preferably from your sales or marketing staff. Next to the subject line, most individuals look at the "from" field before opening an email. The easier it is to identify the sender of an email, the more likely it will be opened.

Subject Line

As previously stated, your subject line is a second chance to make a solid first impression. 35% of email receivers open emails based just on the subject line. If you do not engage here, individuals will not open your email, giving you little chance of converting them. The content of your email can contain the most valuable information in the world, but if the subject line is uninteresting, they will never read it. A few pointers to remember when developing topic lines:

> - *Don't overdo punctuation.*
> - *Keep it short. No more than 40-50 characters.*
> - *Do not use all capitals.*
> - *Do not repeat the "from" label.*

Content

The email's content is its main body. Your preview text sets the tone for everything. Because it adds context and encourages readers to open the email even more, the preview text is your subject line's sidekick. It ought to draw interest and pique curiosity.

The main body of your email should contain the information and messaging that are most important to your readers. The consumer must find value in it and be motivated to act. Make sure everything you're promoting is succinct and presented in an approachable manner, with a connection to your brand voice. Ensure that this content is tailored to the recipient by addressing their specific pain points and offering assistance according to their current stage in the customer journey.

Make a commitment to providing high-quality content that readers will want to read. Fail an email campaign just as easily if your content is tedious or, worse, full of mistakes.

Additionally, the content ought to change. Avoid repeatedly sending out the same campaign. Test topic lines and content with A/B testing to see what works and what doesn't. Next, produce more of it. If you're stumped for ideas for content, the best place to start is usually a company newsletter.

Urge to Take Action

The part of your email where you urge recipients to "do something" is one of the most crucial. This leads to conversion and is known as your call-to-action (CTA). You must include a request for action somewhere in the email, whether you want the recipient to buy something or just complete a survey.

As you write the material, ask yourself, "What do I want readers to do after they receive this"? It is not required to be bought. Don't forget to provide a link for them to complete the survey if one is available.

Making the CTA obvious and succinct is always the goal, as it saves people from having to ponder what to do next. Including a button that is simple to click and takes users directly to your destination is one of the most interesting ways to accomplish this.

Create
Everyone is familiar with the adage "A picture is worth a thousand words". But in terms of email marketing, it remains the same. Sending an email with an image in it plays to the recipient's visual preference. It can break up the written content, add personality to your emails, and facilitate their reception of information.

Visual elements like color blocks and graphics shouldn't be overlooked. Additionally, make sure you consider the general style and arrangement of your emails. A key component of branding is consistency in the look and feel of your visuals, so making sure they match the other digital assets and collateral is essential.

Optimized for Mobile
There's no longer a reason to send emails that aren't mobile-friendly. People's obsession with their phones is already well established, and the fact that up to 77% of emails are opened on mobile devices solidifies the deal. Your emails need to be mobile-friendly. Not only will someone forget to read an email they can't read on their phone, but they might even unsubscribe from receiving any more from you in the future.

Analytical
Your email campaigns should always be quantifiable. Assessing the effectiveness of your email marketing tactics is essential to figuring out what is successful and what is not. A successful email campaign should have high open and click rates; if these metrics aren't being met, it's time to make some adjustments.

Make sure you experiment with A/B testing, the day and time you send your emails, and the frequency when you review your email benchmarks and make changes. All of these have the potential to contribute to overall effectiveness, which is what really counts.

Thus, keep in mind the seven components of the email anatomy listed above when creating your next email newsletter or campaign. Don't prioritize one over the other; successful email requires all of them to work properly.

Chapter 4

Professionalism and Courtesies

Being courteous to others entails treating them with decency and consideration, regardless of their status, role, or viewpoint. It also entails using a clear, succinct, and polished tone, content, and format. Here are some pointers for being polite in emails.

Proper greetings and closings

The way you sign off and address emails can have a significant impact on how they are read. When addressing someone you don't know well, use formal salutations and closings like Dear Mr./Ms./Dr. or Sincerely/Regards. For acquaintances, use casual salutations and closings like "Hello," "Thanks" or "Cheers." Steer clear of using emojis, slang, or acronyms that could come across as impolite or disrespectful.

Language and tone you use

In your emails, your language and tone can express your intentions, attitude, and feelings. Steer clear of words that could offend or hurt your recipients, such as harsh, rude, or sarcastic ones. When expressing your gratitude, admiration, or criticism, use words that are kind, constructive, and positive. Steer clear of using bold fonts, multiple exclamation points, or all caps, as these can come across as demanding or aggressive. Correct spelling, grammar, and punctuation are essential to prevent misunderstandings and confusion.

Succinct and clear

To prevent wasting the time and attention of your recipients, make sure your emails are clear and concise. Make sure your email or memo has a clear, concise subject line that captures the essence of your message or purpose. Make use of concise, straightforward sentences and paragraphs that arrange your thoughts logically and cogently. To draw attention to important ideas or actions, use headings, lists, or bullet points. Steer clear of acronyms, jargon, and technical terms that might be confusing to your audience. Give enough background information and specifics to prevent confusion or misunderstandings.

Expresses Empathy

The more you can sympathize with the subject's concerns, the more likely they are to accept your response, even if it is not what they expected. Expressing your empathy, apologizing for any misunderstanding or difficulty, and giving solutions are all courteous approaches to show the subject that the organization prioritizes their best interests.

This does not require you to send generic emails with no tough messages. A respectful manner in writing, rather than denial and defensiveness, might help you convey a negative message without appearing unduly negative.

Shows appreciation

People want to know that they are valued. It recognizes their existence as human beings and confirms that even the slightest act is not overlooked. Even if a consumer expects nothing in return, expressing your appreciation in writing for just supporting your efforts through their patronage not only inspires continuous loyalty but also sets off a chain reaction of goodwill to others. Never underestimate the power of good manners and politeness in all forms of textual communication.

Respect your recipients' time and privacy

Your emails should respect your receivers' time and privacy. Avoid sending unwanted, irrelevant, or repetitive emails. Avoid sending emails during unsuitable times, such as late at night, early in the morning, or on weekends or holidays. Use the CC and BCC fields correctly to avoid spamming or exposing your recipients' email addresses. Request authorization before forwarding or distributing secret or sensitive material.

Be responsive and courteous

Your emails should be responsive and respectful in order to preserve strong connections and communication with your recipients.

Respond to emails quickly, ideally within 24 hours, or confirm receipt and indicate when you will respond. Please apologize for any interruptions, errors, or inconvenience you may have caused.

Express your gratitude, praise, or compliments when needed. Follow up on any requests, commitments, or feedback you sent or received.

Chapter 5

Selecting the Right Tone

The tone of an email message can communicate your attitude, intention, and expertise to the recipient. Choosing the right tone can help you meet your communication objectives, minimize misunderstandings, and foster great relationships. But how can you choose the right tone for your email message? Here are some suggestions:

Consider your purpose
Why are you sending this email? What do you hope to accomplish? Depending on your goal, you may require a different tone. For example, if you're writing to apologize for a mistake, you might want to employ a humble and genuine tone. If you're writing to urge someone to take action, you might want to utilize a confident and persuasive tone. If you're writing to tell someone of a choice, you should adopt a straightforward and respectful tone.

Know your audience
As previously discussed, to whom are you writing? How well do you know them? What is their relationship with you? How do they expect to be talked to? Depending on your target market, you may need to modify your tone. For example, if you're writing to a coworker or a client, you should employ a formal and professional tone. If you're writing to a friend or family member, you might want to employ a casual and welcoming tone. If you're writing to a stranger or an authority figure, you should use a polite and respectful tone.

Choose your words
The language you use can influence how your message is viewed and received. Depending on the tone you intend to communicate, you may need to use various phrases. For example, if you want to communicate a positive tone, you could use words like thankfulness, admiration, or enthusiasm. If you wish to portray a negative tone, you

can use phrases like dissatisfaction, disappointment, or impatience. If you want to express a neutral tone, use words like factual, objective, or balanced.

Apply punctuation and formatting
The punctuation and formatting you employ can either support or undercut your tone. Depending on the tone you intend to express, you may need to employ various punctuation and formatting. For example, if you want to express a welcoming tone, you could use exclamation marks, emoticons, or informal fonts. If you want to project a serious tone, consider using periods, commas, or formal fonts. If you want to express a clear tone, consider using bullet points, headlines, or bold text.

Read and revise
Reading and rewriting your message can help you identify any faults, inconsistencies, or ambiguities that may impact your tone. Depending on the tone you wish to express, you may need to adjust your message. For example, if you want to communicate in a courteous tone, you should review your spelling, grammar, and punctuation. If you want to communicate a succinct tone, consider removing any unneeded words, sentences, or paragraphs. If you want to establish a consistent tone, make sure your message aligns with your objective, target audience, and words.

Seek feedback
Seeking input from others might help you gain a new perspective on your tone and how it may be perceived by the recipient. Depending on the tone you intend to express, you may need to get input from others. For example, if you want to express a respectful tone, you may need to consult someone who understands the recipient's etiquette and conventions. If you want to portray a persuading tone, consider asking someone who is impartial or suspicious of your point. If you want to communicate in a professional tone, you may wish to consult with someone who has expertise or knowledge in your sector.

Chapter 6

Professional Email Responses

If you have an email marketing list, you need to optimize various aspects to ensure a high return on investment. One of these variables is your email response rate. Your response rates will show you how effective your email marketing campaign is.

Email response rates are the number of email responses you receive after sending out an email campaign. There are various elements that will influence your email response rates. Response rates can be influenced by a variety of factors, including the type of email, your industry, the email platform you use, your target audience, and the email content.

Most marketers aim for a 10% response rate with each email campaign they send out. Depending on the circumstances listed above, this figure could be lower or higher by 5-10%. Your overall response rate will allow you to determine how engaged your email list is with your content.

How to Measure Email Response Rates

Your email response rate is defined by the number of emails that are delivered. A campaign containing 1000 emails could only deliver 950 of them to the recipient's mailbox.

Your email response rate is not solely determined by comparing the amount of email replies with the total amount of emails sent. You would need to examine the number of emails sent vs the number of email answers.

Email response rate = (Emails Delivered ÷ Email Responses gotten) x 100.

To get the number of emails delivered, deduct the number of bounces from the total number of emails sent.

How to Increase Email Response Rates

Get your timing right
The first step in increasing the ROI of your email marketing campaigns and improving response rates is to get the timing right. You must determine the optimal time of day to receive the most clicks.

When it comes to getting your email recipients to open and reply to your messages, you must send them at the appropriate moment.

We will evaluate numerous aspects to improve your timing. First, let's look at some general email send-time tips.

Should you send emails during the day or night? It is better practice to send email campaigns throughout the day rather than at night. Most individuals would be exhausted after work and would just want to unwind. Not checking their emails.

Avoid Mondays
Most marketers advise you to avoid sending out email blasts on Monday. Most individuals would be catching up on work, but their inboxes would also be filled with emails. To avoid your email getting buried in a sea of content, avoid Mondays.

No weekends
Most people spend weekends running errands and relaxing with their family. Weekends have the least open rates compared to weekdays. You should avoid sending emails on weekends.

The best days
According to studies, Tuesdays and Thursdays are ideal days to send out your email newsletter.

Midweek/Mid Day

According to research, the optimum times to send emails are during the middle of the week and around 2 p.m. This intentional timing has been shown to improve email response time, increasing the probability of rapid and timely responses.

The second aspect that influences when you send emails is the recipient's device. User habits vary according to the device they are utilizing. Desktop users should follow the Mid-Week and Mid-Day transmit time restrictions. Mobile users, on the other hand, are active and use their phones well into the evening.

While mobile users are more likely to utilize their devices in the evening, it's worth noting that 41% of email opens occur on mobile devices.

To boost your open and response rates, you need to know which devices your receivers use to read their emails. This will assist you decide on your email outreach plan.

Use a human sender

Always set your sender name to be human. For example, Jane@companyname.com. People are more likely to open emails from humans rather than artificial bots.

If the 'from' name does not sound like it is from someone you want to hear from, the subject line is irrelevant. Do not use the "noreply@company.com" email address. Not only is it not personalized, but individuals cannot add you to their address book. This means that the majority of your emails can end up in the spam folder.

Email Personalization

Email personalization is one of the most effective ways to encourage people to respond to your emails. You could believe that email personalization is simply adding the recipient's name to the email. There are numerous other methods to personalize your emails besides just adding a name. Most readers are already aware of this tactic and may ignore it. Try some of the following tactics in its place:

Use behavior-triggered emails

Behavior-triggered emails are automatic emails delivered to clients depending on how they interact with your product or service.

Emails that are automated are the most personalized email strategy you can employ. They are ideal for welcoming new readers, re-engaging existing customers, and upselling items or services. This type of email allows you to target users based on their preferences and actions.

Monitor the reader's behaviors and interests

This is a more advanced level of customization. You can tailor your email by promoting purchases or activities depending on the reader's past behavior. Amazon makes extensive use of this method.

Understanding your audience's preferences and using that information to create targeted emails should be part of your marketing strategy. Rather than trying to reach out to everyone in your audience with the same emails/promotions, send them emails tailored to their own interests and preferences. This method will help you improve your email response rates.

Include a specific call to action.

Your CTA is the centerpiece of your entire email campaign. It is the factor that affects whether you will reach your campaign's aim, which in this case is to increase your email response rate. If you aren't already optimizing your email CTAs, you should start today. Here are some great practices to optimize your email CTA.

Choose the appropriate placements.
Your CTA should be plainly apparent to the reader. Whether the recipient is on a tablet, mobile phone, or desktop, you should place your CTA button where it is easily visible.

Placing the CTA button alongside a visually appealing image is a good idea. This would enhance the likelihood of the reader seeing the CTA. For example, Ally places the "Learn more" CTA button next to a well-designed graphic. You'll see that the CTA button is in easy-to-read typefaces that stand out against the rest of the picture content on the screen.

Use action-oriented terms
Use action-oriented language that will elicit a specific response from the recipient. Use CTA buttons like "Get Exclusive Tips" and "Try For Free" instead of keywords like "Read More".

Use the correct colors
Color can greatly influence the recipient's decision to conduct a specific action. In an ocean of content marketing, color can help your message stand out. It is what causes your target audience to see what you want them to see, experience what you want them to feel, and act as you want them to.

You should choose appropriate colors to grab the reader's attention. To increase involvement, make your CTA button stand out from the rest of the text and backdrop colors.

Have a clear value proposition

To enhance email response rates, you should clearly demonstrate the benefits that recipients will receive from interacting with your email. A value proposition is a brief statement that describes the benefits of adopting a product or service. In the case of an email, it explains why the reader should take action.

First, it explains to the reader what the product provides, and then tells them the benefits they would obtain from using the software to write emails. Your value proposition is really crucial. It directs the reader to do a specific action. If you don't clearly demonstrate your value proposition, you may have reduced the likelihood of the reader clicking on your CTA button.

When writing a value proposition, it should meet three fundamental requirements:

Clarity
Your value proposition should be worded in a way that clearly communicates what the product can achieve for customers. Refrain from using marketing lingo or buzzwords.

Benefits
A great value proposition concentrates on the benefits the reader will receive from the product.

Differentiation
Your value proposition must set your items or services apart from the competition. You should explain explicitly why your product is the best option for them.

Be as brief as possible
Most readers have a brief attention span, so go right to the point. If you cannot capture the readers' interest within the first two lines of your email, you will lose them.

Your email should take no more than 30 seconds to read. Anything more than that, and they will most certainly lose interest.
To increase your chances of receiving a response, indicate how you can resolve their issues as soon as feasible.

Comply with CAN-SPAM rules

You will not receive any response or engagement if your emails end up in the spam folder. To ensure that your emails arrive in the reader's inbox, observe CAN-SPAM standards.

CAN-SPAM (Controlling the Assault of Non-Solicited Pornography And Marketing) is a law that specifies the regulations for commercial email and promotional messages, allows receivers the opportunity to have a firm cease emailing them, and outlines the penalties incurred for those who break the law. To comply, below are certain regulations to follow:

DO

> - *Include your physical postal address in all emails.*
> - *Give a clear unsubscribe button, and you must comply within 10 business days.*
> - *Use "From", "To", and "Reply to" wording that clearly identifies you.*

DON'T

> - *Do not sell people's email addresses from your subscription list.*
> - *You cannot ask a receiver to pay a price, provide further information, or browse a single page on a website before unsubscribing.*
> - *Avoid using false subject lines that differ from the content of your communication.*

Proofread

This may sound obvious, but you would be surprised how many individuals do not proofread their emails before sending them. Make sure your emails are free of spelling problems and poor language.

Grammar or spelling errors may make you appear unprofessional and reduce your email response rates. Your goal should be to provide the finest possible experience for the reader.

Chapter 6

Dealing With Email Overload

Staying on top of your email might feel like a full-time job, what with screening through spam, creating appropriate responses, and keeping track of messages that require follow-up. That's why we tapped the brains of pros who have discovered the key to effective, organized inboxes despite receiving hundreds of emails per day. Because having a structure in place can help you manage even the most chaotic inbox. Emails that call for quick action should only be kept in your inbox.

Zero mail may be an unrealistic goal, but by being rigorous about which messages take up space in your inbox, you may get quite close.

Most days, my email inbox has under thirty messages. This is deliberate. I want to be able to open my inbox and immediately see what is the most important and requires a response. This practice encourages me to act on stuff in an exceptionally timely manner.

It is not uncommon to receive over 100 emails in a matter of hours, many of which are urgent and involve high-level management.

Create a Waiting Folder
Create a waiting folder for emails that require someone else to take action before you can react. This is a significant time saver because those emails won't clutter up your inbox, and it's a fantastic spot to check every day or week to remind you of what assignments are still outstanding. I spent half a day searching for that email among the many that were in my mailbox at the time. I determined to take control of my inbox from that point on.

Labels

Email labels are your buddy; use them to bundle key email chains so that you can simply find something for reference. I have dozens of subfolders with hundreds of emails stored for future reference. I can find what I need within seconds of a request since I know where it is stored and how to get to it quickly.

Set Filters

Many email providers allow you to create inbox rules or filters that will take action for you and help you rapidly categorize emails without tiring your mental capacity. I've set up rules to sort emails into different categories, color code them, and prioritize them based on the sender. At the end of the day, the rules ensure that I am continually following up and blocking noise. This aids in minimizing the clutter for me.

Track emails that require follow-up

Because some emails may require more than a basic response. If I receive an email that requires both an instant answer and some form of follow-up action, I transfer it to a specified subfolder and set a reminder on my calendar with the folder location and the date when the follow-up is due.

Create templates for your go-to responses

Tailoring a distinct response for each email can be extremely time-consuming. If you find yourself sending the same type of email again and over, consider keeping some stock responses in your drafts that you are able to reuse.

Set aside time blocks for checking emails.

You wouldn't leave your schedule open for meetings at random times and lengths around the clock, so why let email intrude on your day?

I plan specific times during the day to read through each email and wisely react, archive, or save for later. I don't just leave my email open all day. This way, I don't multitask and can get through all of my emails faster because I'm focused on the topic at hand. I recommend that people begin with three different half-hour chunks per day to read and answer their emails, keeping their inbox closed for the remainder of the day, and adapt as needed from there.

Turn off email notifications
Even if you've resigned yourself to simply checking emails in predetermined intervals, the siren call of your inbox notification may be too tempting to refuse. If that's the case, the solution is straightforward: Turn off notifications. If you work in time blocks, you won't go more than a few hours without checking your emails. Turn off notifications because they will distract you from what you are currently working on at your computer.

Squeeze in mindless email tasks during downtime
Ensure that your email accounts are properly connected to your phone, and use downtime to undertake fast inbox cleanup. Sometimes the communications I receive do not necessitate immediate action. Spam can be deleted, other items can be filed, and you can handle a lot of these while waiting in line at the grocery for two minutes.

Conclusion

When drafting an email, it is critical to get right to the point. The recipient should comprehend the email's objective within seconds. To ensure that your emails are clear and concise, keep them short and to the point, utilize bullet points as needed, and avoid using technical jargon that the receiver may not be familiar with.

It is also crucial to consider the recipient's point of view. Consider what information they require and how you can deliver it in the most efficient manner. This will allow you to compose emails that are not only clear and succinct but also effective in accomplishing their intended goal.

The subject line of an email is frequently the first thing the receiver sees, so it is critical to figure out whether the email will be opened or not. When drafting subject lines, keep them short and to the point, and ensure that they appropriately reflect the email's content.

It is also vital to avoid using false subject lines since they can harm your professional reputation and cause the reader to lose trust in your emails. Additionally, avoid using all caps or unreasonable punctuation, which can come out as spammy.

Writing Professional Emails With Results

Writing professional emails is an important component of communication in today's corporate world. Whether you're sending an email to a coworker, a client, or a supervisor, the subject matter and tone of your message can have a big impact on your relationships and ability to fulfill your objectives. There are several crucial things to consider when writing successful, professional emails that produce results.

First and foremost, make your messages clear and succinct. This means avoiding long, meandering sentences and getting right to the point. Begin your email by clearly defining the aim of your letter, and use bullet points or numbered lists to divide complex information into small bits. This not only makes your message easy to read, but it also allows your recipient to swiftly grasp what you're attempting to convey.

Email etiquette is also a significant concern. This involves using a professional email signature, proper salutations, and closing lines, and avoiding slang or informal language. It's also crucial to consider tone when composing emails; while it's fine to be nice and personable, you should always keep a professional demeanor.

When writing your emails, keep your target audience in mind. Who are you sending the message to, and what information do they need? What are their objectives and concerns? By making the effort to study your target audience, you can personalize your messaging to fit their needs and boost the likelihood that your email will be positively received.

Finally, before sending an email, make sure you proofread it carefully. Typos, grammatical errors, and other problems can diminish the professionalism of your communication and create the appearance that you aren't paying attention to detail. Take a few extra moments to thoroughly study your message before clicking "send" to ensure that it is polished and error-free.

Creating effective emails requires careful attention to detail and knowledge of the best practices for this kind of writing. By being precise, succinct, and conscious of your audience and tone, you can create effective and professional communications that will help you achieve your objectives and build good connections with your coworkers, clients, and supervisors.

Writing an Effective Email Introduction

The introduction to an email is the first opportunity to capture the recipient's attention and express the goal of the communication. To write a successful beginning, clearly describe the aim of the email and provide a brief summary of the content.

Additionally, it is critical to establish a connection with the recipient by greeting them by name and expressing gratitude for their time and attention. This will help to set a good tone for the rest of the email, increasing the likelihood of the person receiving it engaging with its content.

The Art of Creating the Perfect Email Signature

Your email signature is a crucial aspect of your email and is sometimes the first thing recipients see after reading your message. It is an opportunity to make a positive impression and leave a lasting impression on your recipient. Here are some tips for creating the ideal email signature:

Keep things simple
A clean, uncomplicated signature is more effective than a cluttered one. Maintain your name, work title, and contact details.

Include your company's name
This is especially vital if you're representing a business or group. It reinforces your brand and adds context to the recipient.

Include a professional headshot
Including a professional headshot in your signature will help you personalize your emails and make a powerful first impression.

Use your brand's colors
Using your brand colors in your signature is an excellent approach to strengthen your brand identification. This can be as basic as adding your brand's color to your name or as complex as designing a full-color signature with your corporate logo.

Add social media links

If you have busy social media accounts, consider including links in your signature. This allows your recipient to communicate with you on multiple platforms.

Stay consistent

Make sure your signature is in line with your overall brand and messaging. This will help to strengthen your brand and create a lasting impression.

Make it mobile-friendly

With the growing usage of mobile devices to check email, it's critical to ensure your signature is mobile-friendly. This means it should be simple to read and navigate on small screens.

By following these guidelines, you can develop a professional and distinctive email signature that will leave a lasting impression on your recipients.

How To Write Effective Follow-Up Emails

Although follow-up emails are a crucial part of business correspondence, they can be challenging to write properly. The following tips will help you write a great follow-up email:

Don't write too much

Email follow-ups must be succinct and uncomplicated. It's likely that your recipient is preoccupied and lacks the time to peruse an extended message.

Act civil

Email follow-ups ought to be polite and courteous at all times. Don't be confrontational or make demands.

Give some background

Be sure to provide context in your email follow-up. This gives the recipient the information they need to reply and enables them to comprehend the email's purpose.

Give details

Make it clear to the recipient what you're following up on and what action you want them to take. This will help them understand what you're asking of them and facilitate their response.

Concisely phrase your topic line

Make sure your email's subject line is concise and accurately sums up what's within. This makes it easier for your recipient to recognize and order your messages.

Have patience

It could take some time to hear back from follow-up emails. Have patience and refrain from following up with too many emails too quickly. This could be perceived as hostile, which would be detrimental to your rapport with the recipient.

You can write excellent follow-up emails that are considerate, knowledgeable, and useful by using these tips.

Proofreading Emails Before Sending Them Is Crucial

You should edit your emails before sending them for a number of reasons. The first and most important advantage is that it keeps you from making embarrassing errors or typos that will give you a less-than-professional appearance. Additionally, it lets you check your message for errors or inconsistencies, which might assist make sure that it is understood correctly.

Before sending an email, give it another read, especially if it's to a person of importance like your boss or a possible client. It shows that you value the recipient's time and take email communication seriously when you take the extra time to proofread your work.

Read your emails through from start to finish while proofreading them. This will enable you to find any mistakes or typos that could have slipped your mind during the first writing of the email. To identify any mistakes you might have overlooked when reading the email silently, try reading it loudly.

Make sure your email is formatted correctly and that any spelling and grammar errors are corrected. To make your email look professional and easy to read, you should assess the font, spacing, and margins.

How to Use Email to Leave a Positive First Impression

Sending a stranger an email is a great way to establish rapport and create a positive first impression. Make a good first impression by staying professional, courteous, and succinct while emailing a stranger.

Start your email with a succinct salutation that outlines the message's goal. Then, tell the recipient what they need to know by getting right to the point. To help the receiver understand why you are sending the email, be sure to include any relevant information. For example, include the email's purpose.

Be cautious to be professional and kind when sending an email to someone you don't know. To avoid making the receiver defensive and less likely to respond to your email, avoid using wording that could be perceived as hostile or demanding.

Make sure your email is clear and easy to read before sending it to a stranger. This entails proofreading your email for errors in syntax and spelling and making sure it is formatted correctly.

How to Write Emails with Professionalism and Respect

Sending an email can be challenging since you want to convey your message effectively while also exhibiting professionalism and respect. Whether you're sending an update, asking for a break, or seeking clarification on a project, you should take the time to write your email in a kind and professional manner. Here are some ideas:

First and foremost, make sure your message is written in a professional manner. This entails speaking in a more somber and businesslike tone and staying away from slang, emoticons, and extremely informal language. To avoid coming out as confrontational or rude, use caution while speaking about sensitive or possibly contentious subjects.

Get straight to the point and state your email's purpose from the outset. To break up complex information into manageable chunks, utilize numbered lists or bullet points rather than long, rambling sentences. This helps you understand what you're trying to communicate right away and makes your message easier to read.

It's also important to take into account their priorities and time while sending emails. When sending your email, think about the best time to do so and make sure it is pertinent and significant. Instead of just checking in via email, concentrate on providing information that is essential to the task at hand or the decision-making process.

Finally, make sure you thoroughly proofread an email before sending it. Grammar mistakes, typos, and other issues might make your message seem less professional and as though you aren't paying close attention to details. Spend a few more minutes proofreading your message to make sure it is flawless and free of errors before pressing "send."

Email communication requires a careful balancing act between professionalism, decency, and directness. By being mindful of your tone and language, being clear and concise in your messaging, and showing consideration for the recipient's time and priorities, you may create emails that show off your professionalism and assist you in reaching your objectives.

Rules of Email Etiquette That Everyone Should Adhere to:

> ➤ *Answer emails right away.*
> ➤ *Make use of a business email address.*
> ➤ *Steer clear of exclamation points and uppercase characters.*
> ➤ *Before mailing, proofread.*
> ➤ *Keep your voice polite and respectful.*

Maintaining business partnerships requires proper email etiquette. Instantaneously replying to emails shows the receiver that you value their time and are aware of their needs. It also makes it simpler for people to identify and get in touch with you if you use a business email address that has your name and other pertinent details.

Additionally, it's critical to refrain from using a lot of capital letters or exclamation points in your emails as this could come across as unpleasant or hostile. Take a few minutes to review every email before sending it to make sure it is error-free, concise, and clear. Lastly, regardless of the recipient or subject matter of your emails, always write in a courteous and professional manner.

One of the most important skills for interacting more effectively and professionally at work is writing outstanding emails. Making better emails and leaving a better impression on clients, bosses, and coworkers can be achieved by using the strategies and advice in this book. Taking the time to craft a well-thought-out email that clearly conveys your message is essential, regardless of whether you're sending it to a coworker or your boss on a business note. By keeping these tips in mind, you may send emails that are concise, effective, and clear, improving your ability to communicate and forging stronger bonds with coworkers.